100 Japanese Stencil Designs

Edited by
Friedrich Deneken

Dover Publications, Inc.
Mineola, New York

Note

For centuries, Japanese artists have been renowned for the subtlety, ingenuity and acute artistic sensibility of their designs. They have evolved these qualities in the course of a long-lived artistic tradition that often focuses on plants, birds, flowers, fish, grasses and other natural elements. With seemingly effortless skill, the artist recaptures their beauty and delicacy, and presents them in dense, intricately balanced patterns. This mastery is wonderfully evident in this collection of 100 stencil designs, reprinted from a rare 19th-century German portfolio. Depicted here in styles ranging from realistic to deeply stylized, are such familiar Japanese motifs as peonies, bamboo rods, pine branches, dragons, carnations, chrysanthemums, cranes, carp, lilies, and other plants and animals in a profusion of eye-catching tableaux. Artists, craftspeople and any lover of Japanese art will treasure this abundant supply of authentic, ready-to-use stencil designs.

Bibliographical Note

This Dover edition, first published in 2006, is an original selection of plates, slightly reduced in size, from *Japanische Motive Für Flächenverzierung: Ein Formenschatz Für Das Kunstgewerbe,* published by Verlag von Julius Becker: Berlin, 1897. Plates 3, 14, 18, 83, 92, 94, and 98 of the original have been omitted from this edition, along with the foreword and introduction. A Note and new English translations of the original German captions have been specially prepared for this volume.

DOVER *Pictorial Archive* SERIES

This book belongs to the Dover Pictorial Archive Series. You may use the designs and illustrations for graphics and crafts applications, free and without special permission, provided that you include no more than four in the same publication or project. (For permission for additional use, please write to Permissions Department, Dover Publications, Inc., 31 East 2nd Street, Mineola, N.Y. 11501.)

However, republication or reproduction of any illustration by any other graphic service, whether it be in a book or in any other design resource, is strictly prohibited.

International Standard Book Number: 0-486-44724-3

Manufactured in the United States of America
Dover Publications, Inc., 31 East 2nd Street, Mineola, N.Y. 11501

1. **Carp Swimming in Waves**

2. A Pair of Cranes in Pine Branches

3. A Cherry Tree in Bloom

4. Peony Blooms and Buds

5. **Bamboo, Camellias, and Sparrows**

6. **Pine Needles and Buds on a Rocky Ground**

7. **Bamboo Rods, Pine Needles on Snow Rosettes and Circular Cranes (Symbols of Luck)**

8. **Rosette-Shaped Young Pine Motifs (With Roots) Situated among Ferns (Symbol of the New Year)**

9. **Floral Motifs on Cloud Background**

10. Cranes and Autumnal Reeds

11. Bridge Patterns in a Swamp of Irises

12. Wickerwork; Matching Stencil
Pair for Two-Tone Decoration

13. Blooming Branches of a Kiri Tree (*Paulownia imperialis*)

14. Karakusa: Stylized Chrysanthemums in a Chinese Style

15. Carnations in Bloom

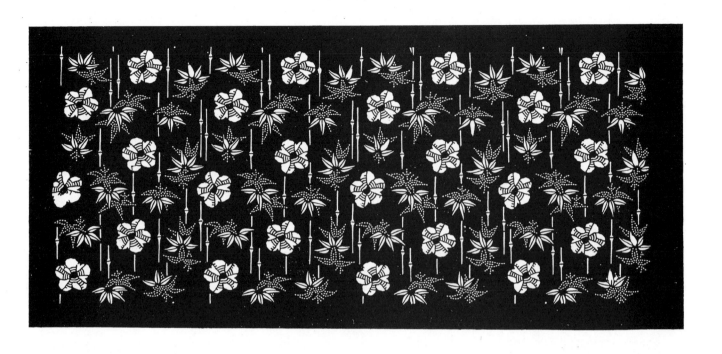

16. **Bamboo and Mum Blooms** 17. **Hishi Blooms on a Diamond-Scored Background**

18. Branches of the Hanging Cherry Tree (Blooms with Various Inner Patterns); Fans with Swallows, Clouds with Cross Patterns

19. **Straw-Roofed Houses in a Bamboo Thicket**

20. **Nets Hung Out to Dry; Waves**

21. Dragon in a Swirl of Clouds

22. Peony Blooms

23. Bamboo Rods and Shapes Containing Floral Motifs

24. Butterflies on a Background of Dotted Clouds

25. Grapevines

26. Wild Geese and Reeds

27. Hexagonal Fields with Blooms and Basic Patterns (In Karakusa Style)

28. Peony Blooms with Lightly Scored Background

29. Bamboo Rods

30. Small Snow Rosettes with Pine Needles and Mums

31. Pine Branches

32. Sword Lilies

33. **Monochoria, Okra Flowers, Hagi Branches**

34. Coltsfoot

35. **Hydrangea and Carnations**

36. Radishes

37. Gourds

38. Maple Branches

39. Pine Branches and Spotted Bamboo Rods

40. Well Openings Containing the Character "Tatsu" (Dragon)

41. Fish in a Whirlpool

42. Butterflies and Hagi Branches

43. Cherry Blooms with a Stripe Pattern

44. Star Pattern with Floral Motifs

45. Mum Blooms with Diagonal Stripes

46. Pine, Bamboo, and Mums in Snow

47. Peony Flowers

48. Swallows in Maple Branches

49. Falcons in Pine Branches

50. Swallows in Rain

51. Iris Swamp

52. Waves

53. Wild Geese in Waves

54. Torn Ginkgo Leaves with Vetch Tendrils

55. Nightingales in a Blooming Mum Tree

56. Nandina and Sparrows

57. **Glycine Flowers with Pairs of Written Characters (Meaning "Nine")**

58. Vetch Tendrils

59. Wild Geese Flying Over Susuki Grass

60. Blooming Sword Lilies

61. Bamboo Trees

62. Old Bamboo Rods

63. Pine

64. Swallows and Weeping Willows

65. Lobsters

66. Butterflies

67. Butterflies and Chrysanthemums

68. Snow (In Rosette Form), Mum Flowers, Pine Needles

69. Blooming Cherry Branches

70. Swallows, Footballs, and Willow Rods

71. Swimming Carp, Goldfish, and Trout

72. Ominaeshi (An Autumn Plant)

73. Peonies and Bamboo Rods

74. Blooming Hibiscus

75. Coltsfoot

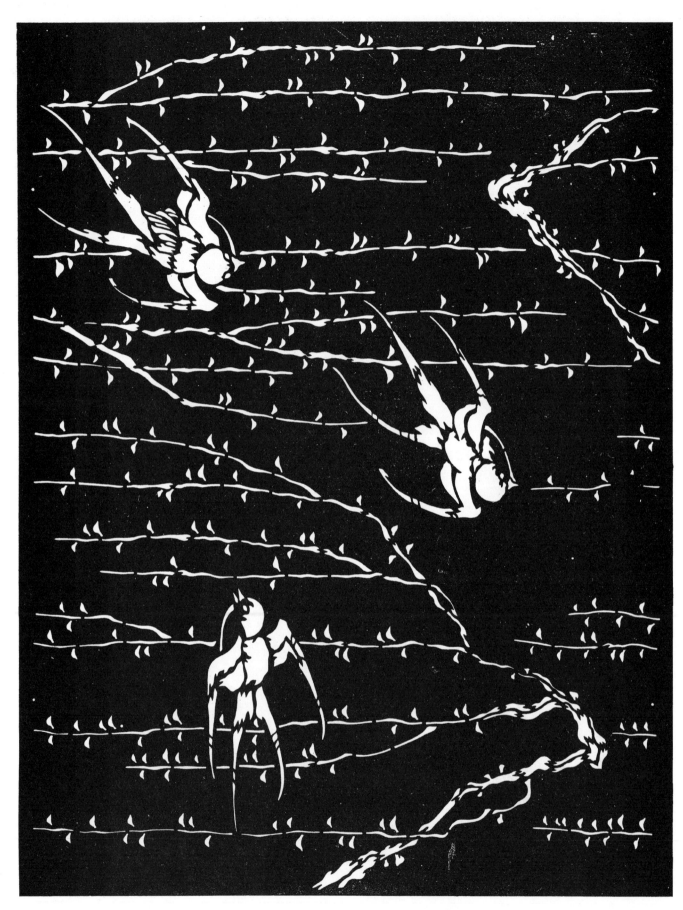

76. Weeping Willow and Swallows

77. Morning Glories on Bamboo Rods

78. Butterflies and Susuki Grass

79. Vine Tendrils and Bamboo Rods

80. Fall Motif: Ginkgo Leaves, Maple Branches, Blades of Grass (With Dew) and Wild Geese over an Island with Pine Trees and Fields

81. Lobsters

82. Pine Branches with Cones

83. Vines on a Diagonally Striped Background

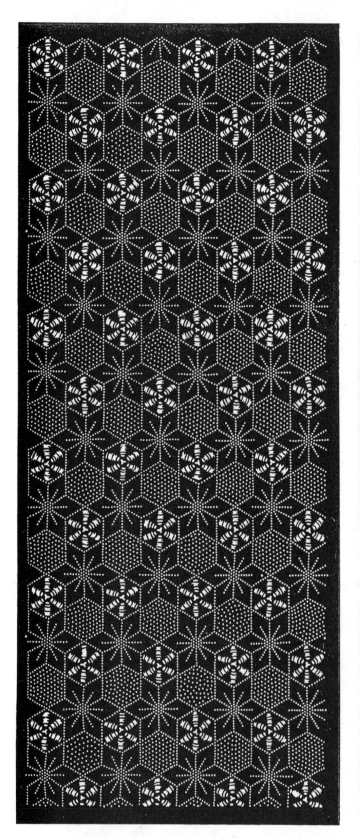

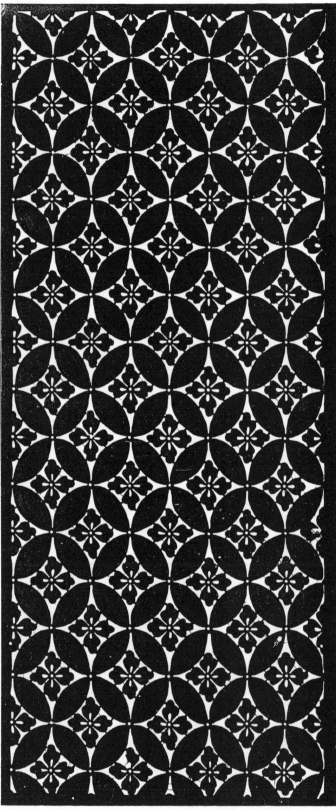

**84. Star Pattern with
Snow Flowers**

**85. "Shippo" Pattern (Overlapping
Circles) with Hishi Flowers**

86. Swimming Carp

87. Wild Geese over Water and Chenopodium Plants

88. Eggplant (*Solanum melongena*)

89. **Quail in Hagi Bushes**

90. Cranes in Water and in a Pine Tree by the Shore

91. Torn Banana Leaves

92. Roses, Carnations, Sparrows

93. Clematis

94. Blooming Cherry Flowers

95. Dying Cedar Trees

96. **Pine and Climbing Plants ("Tsuta")**

97. Glycine Leaves

98. Vines

99. Peach Branches and Cherry Blooms　　　**100. Bamboo with Braided Patterns**

101. Written on Slates with Pencils and Chrysanthemum